Michael Norton

I0416346

CONTENTS

Chapter#1
1966 – 1972

In regards to this transgender person knowledge was scarce and wisdom was lacking. There are children that contended from the time they could speak that they were not the sex which they were assigned at birth. Gender isn't necessarily our genitalia rather it comes from our brain where we alone know our true selves. Brains have been studied and shown to resemble the gender which the person is trying to tell others that they truly are. We need to open our ears and hear what these individuals are telling us. Dysphoria is very real and should not be looked at lightly in any regard.

I was born in 1966 which wasn't a good year for a girl with a penis. In 1966 a man who underwent a sex reassignment surgery had wanted to change their name but was denied by the New York City Health Department. It is no small thing to say that we have come a long way since then. One can now change their name and sex as long as they've had the proper surgery. The Creator alone knows how many times I have prayed to wake up in a female body. Not that I didn't know that it wouldn't happen overnight as such but I strongly felt the desire for change.

Back when I was a child there was a conflict that arose over being a transsexual. I like the sound of the Black Cat Tavern but I don't like what happened there in 1967. That Los Angeles club was raided by twelve plain clothes police officers. People were beaten and arrests of patrons and employees alike were made. Later there were protests which were organized by P.R.I.D.E. or Personal Rights in Defense and Education. That was the first use of the word pride which is now associated with the LGBTQ community. Let's discuss this pride a little further.

A man named Gilbert Barker designed the rainbow pride flag and it was waved on June 25th, 1978. That happened at the San Francisco gay freedom-day and each color had a meaning assigned to it. Purple was for spirit, indigo was for serenity, turquoise was magic, green for nature, yellow for sunlight, orange for healing, red for life and hot pink stood for sex. But in 1979 turquoise was removed leaving us with the flag that we have today. It is 2022 and we have come a long way since 1966.

But my personal question is besides knowing myself to have been a girl all along, was it merely a Y-chromosome that had them assign me as a male at birth? The answer to that surprisingly might be "no!" The Y-chromosome holds only 60 genes whereas the X-chromosome has 900. And over 17,000 men in America don't even have a Y-chromosome. Whereas some women do. I don't want to get into science here this was just something to mention because the answers have yet to be solidified. But, if you do simple research on chromosomes, you will find that they don't make up gender just bodily aspects.

Let's talk a little about dysphoria, I had it bad as a child and it affected every aspect of my life. But I can remember one day that was seared into my mind and I'll tell you what it was. When I was about 4 or 5 my mother had taken me out shopping with her and one of the stops was a dress shop. I was thrilled just walking in there with all of the dresses that I saw. I can remember giddy about being there. My mother had gone off on her own to look for whatever she was there for and I was running around on my own.

There was another woman who had what I would imagine was her daughter with her maybe about 18 years old. I waited for the girl to turn around and then ran up and smacked her on the ass then quickly shoved my way through some dresses on a long rack to where I couldn't be seen on the other side. Then I stealthily followed them until I was able to run up and smack her on the ass, again disappearing into a rack of dresses. I had gotten away with it twice but on the third try she spun around and grabbed me up in the air telling me that she had me.

I forget so much of my past but that memory of simply shopping in a dress store has stayed with me all of my years. I even kept that day s a running fantasy and too had dreams about it. I even thought about how the girl that had picked me up had been wearing blue-jeans and had it been me I would have preferred a dress. They were probably there to buy one for an occasion but to me every day was a suitable occasion for the wearing of a dress. I still feel the same but we're getting to that part. For now, I am going over my history and struggles with dysphoria.

You might have wondered why I didn't say "I am a girl." Well, I said "Me a girl" because it comes from a real point in time. A little childish but then I was only around 5 at the time. I had been out shopping with my mother and we had just gotten home. As she was keying the lock on the front door, I looked up at her and proclaimed "Me a girl!" She merely looked down and smiled at me then walked into the house and went out of sight. I remember feeling that my statement had been important to me but it hadn't gotten so much as a comment. It was something that I'll never forget.

I know that it is not uncommon for little girls to say that they are a boy when engaging in boy's games or for little boys to say that they are girls but none of that comes out of dysphoria. In the vast majority of cases, they are simply ignorant children voicing some current confusion. They simply forget all about it and get on with their lives. For truly dysphoric children the opposite is true they don't forget about it and they don't simply get on with their lives. Most likely they suffer symptoms that are likened to depression.

I know first hand what being dysphoric is like and it isn't a comfortable feeling to have. One can't simply escape those feelings either they are ever present. And for me it was even worse as I had to attend kindergarten at a Catholic school. All of the girls wore skirts and there was something different about their shirts too but I can't remember what exactly. All I know is that I spent a lot of time staring at them with what was probably an envious eye.

I couldn't feel like I belonged anywhere except when I was alone and that used to get to me. I was partially growing up anti-social and that caused feelings of loneliness in me. Back then we had nothing on television about being transgender at least nothing that I ever saw. And, of course, there were no computers to research and learn about things on. I really didn't care for the seventies too much but things did change toward the end of them but that is for later. Right now, I am concentrating on the early seventies.

There is a picture of me and my sister sitting on either side of my uncle Paul, my dad's twin brother at Christmas. Paul was a Catholic priest and used to conduct Christmas mass right in the house at the dinner table before we ate. Anyway, in that picture, besides my short haircut I look just like some little girl in posture as I leaned on him. I still find it to be a disturbing photograph but I have yet to destroy it. And no, my uncle never touched my sister or I in any inappropriate manner. And then there was the time that I wanted to see someone else naked to see if they looked like me. A boy my age who lived in the neighborhood was at the house and we were down in the basement playing. I asked him if he would go around the corner of a wall and take his clothes off and said that I would do the same. He did and when he came walking up to me naked, I stared at his phallus and saw that it looked just like mine. That was it we quickly got dressed and never talked about it again. I don't know if he was dysphoric or gay or just playing around but he had followed my lead to the letter.

But then we moved from Virginia when my father got a promotion at work. He had been promoted to general manager at AT&T and we moved to a place called Timonium Maryland. I remember him calling me tiger, the tiger of Timonium. We moved into a nice middle class house in a very quiet and somewhat upper-class neighborhood. I loved my new bedroom except for the fact that it was over the garage and I would wake up when somebody would open the garage door and start up the car. But I had picked out the room so I wasn't exactly complaining.

I believe that I have said enough about my early childhood so I will type out one more paragraph and then move on to my teenaged years. They say that if feelings of dysphoria persist for more than six months then you are transgender or something along those lines.   Mine had persisted all throughout my childhood so you know that I had it bad. But the true hell really started as I neared puberty. I didn't want to become like my father or any man for that matter. I felt like I was doomed.

Chapter#2
The Wasted Years

In Timonium there was a secular school within walking distance of the house so that's where I was sent. My dysphoria continued as was usual but the older the girls got the more despondent, I became. I would play with other children but not really make friends with them. School did have some good days though like the day I won the first writing contest. I have no idea why they chose my story it was about a guy with a long knife that went around slashing people. But after I read it out loud it won the contest. That's when I first thought about being an author.

One day when I was about 10 there was nobody home and I knew that no one would be for at least an hour. I had an older sister only two years older and just about my size so I went into her bedroom to try on one of her dresses. It was something that I had wanted to do for quite some time but there was normally somebody around. I pulled out a purple dress from her closet and eagerly put it on and it fit me perfectly. It was an exhilarating feeling to not only be feeling the softness of the dress but just to finally have worn one blew my mind. I walked barefoot in that dress all over the house and was having a grand old time doing it.

One thing that I made into a habit was taking late night strolls around the neighborhood or down at the school. I would sneak out of the house after midnight when, as far as I knew, the neighbors were all asleep. If I was going to walk around the neighborhood then I would go to the side of the house and take off all of my clothes and then climb over the fence and just walk naked into the night. Usually, I would walk right up the middle of the streets but sometimes I would walk around on someone's lawn. I loved taking naked walks it made me feel free somehow.

But what I really enjoyed was walking down to the school and then leaving my clothes in the woods while I walked all around the grounds. I liked playing on the swings and feeling the sand between my toes in the playground sandbox. I always knew that the janitor's car was parked there but I never did see anyone so I didn't care. And I had to be one of a kind because after years

5

of taking late night strolls I had never seen anyone else out doing it. Oh, and in the summer, they had a stream that I could walk in and cool myself off. But I wasn't masturbating because I didn't care for that.

I was sitting on the floor in my bedroom when I was twelve and playing with some toy soldiers which is an old school thing to have done. I had an ex-military father and he loved buying me soldiers and forts and things like that. Anyway, when I had been much younger, I used to have an imaginary friend called the Easter Bunny. One day I just stopped talking to them out loud when others were around. But I would still speak to them from time to time even when I was twelve. Believe it or not it was as if they answered me too.

I was playing with knights invading a castle and I had wished that I had a chariot like I had seen on TV. During the month I had smoked marijuana like three times with some local teenaged girls but hadn't gotten high yet. I asked my imaginary friend what it would be like if I got stoned as they call it. The answer I got was this. "You'll hear a loud booming." I got back to playing with my knights and forgot all about the marijuana. But I still wanted a chariot on my floor.

Late in the afternoon one day I was sitting in some 15-year-old girl's bedroom smoking out of a little purple bong. Her bedroom walls were painted black and she had a painting on the wall. The painting was of an ocean wave cresting with four horses running on the wave. I had kept looking at it and too I was high for the first time and felt really funny. When I left her house, it was dark and I had to walk like nine houses down a hill to get to my street. Our house was at the bottom of the hill looking straight up it. I remember feeling uncoordinated as I walked down the hill and when I reached the house there were cars parked there.

Of all nights there were two car loads of relatives from New Jersey visiting us. Well, no one of the cars belonged to my uncle Paul who lived in Washington, DC. Anyway, I stood up in the kitchen overlooking the family room and claimed that I wasn't feeling well and needed to lay down. I was excused to go lay down and went straight to my bedroom and fell out upon my bed. I was feeling dizzy and just needed to close my eyes and wait for the high to wear off. Being stoned I had gotten on the bed backwards with my head at the bottom. It mustn't have taken long for me to fall asleep.

I was looking down at bright blue that was full of golden five-pointed stars. All of the stars suddenly rushed away to my left and I saw the blue roll up from right to left like it was a scroll. But there was still blue there and then the scene widened and I saw a chariot. Four white horses pulling a chariot with a gold-plated front. And upon the chariot I saw a white-haired male wearing light blue and white with a golden breastplate. And he was riding directly at me but it happened in sequences like four of them getting closer each time.

When the chariot was just about where it would have ridden over me it suddenly turned to its right leaving a left profile visible to me. And he raised his left hand up in the air and I think that he snapped his fingers. All at once I heard a very loud booming sound and then I watched as he rode away out of sight. Then everything went dark, pitch black. Except I saw what I guess was me sitting on an oval shaped stone atop of another stone for its base. It tipped and I fell off and was falling through the darkness. Then I stopped falling and was stretched out arms and legs spread and I started spinning.

When I woke up my head was hanging down over the foot of the bed. It's no wonder that I had thought that I was falling. And that charioteer looked just like Zeus. I'm not sure about the stars or scroll but I certainly did hear a loud booming. Anyway, I had only smoked marijuana because I wanted to hang out with the girl and that was her thing. Trying to interpret the dream would be pointless I wanted a chariot and I heard a loud booming. And the gold stars that went away were probably all the good grades that I wouldn't be getting now that I was a pot head.

After that night I learned that I could hang out with a group of teenaged girls as long as I was smoking pot. The only problem was that I was having a bad reaction to it because it caused me to become totally quiet and just stare at things. Like catatonic is how I would describe it. Other people would be talking but I would just be there and completely out of it. The girls were supposed to help with my dysphoria but the pot was ruining everything. Then one day I decided to go for a long walk across town.

I was walking and I met some guy riding his bicycle around some stores. We talked for a little while and then I asked him if he wanted to get high. It was summer and I would be starting seventh grade in a new school in like a month so making friends was a good idea. He lived right up the street so we went to the house and up to his bedroom to get high. I found that I wasn't as reserved with him when I was stoned, I could talk to him and even joke around. He turned out to be my best friend all throughout my school years.

When school began, I had the one friend and we learned that people partied up on a hill before school so we went up there. After partying with people on the hill we all became a click and we were the stoners in the school. Then next came the parties and even more people were known to me. I had lost touch with my dysphoria as I was now either stoned or drunk or both nearly every woke hour of the day. That is until my seat got switched in science class. I was to take a seat in the back of the room next to a girl with very well shaped breasts and in the middle of her puberty.

It had to be her pheromones because every day like clock-work, I got a hardon sitting next to that girl. Sometimes after class I would have to wait for everyone else to leave because I was hard. Or I had to put my binder in front of my pants to hide the obvious boner. She was what I wanted to be, I wanted to be experiencing her puberty not mine. I never did get up the courage to ask her out but she used to drive me nuts just sitting there. One day I was simply too high to face anybody so I asked to go to the nurse's office and went there. The girl known as the most popular and foxy came walking in and stood over me. "Is something wrong?" she said. God did I want to tell her the truth.

I was partying all the time and getting laid on a regular basis by a few different girls but I was also fucking up my program really badly. I ended up really liking LSD and started eating it all the time. One night while tripping I was arrested. The night before court I went into a doughnut shop like a dumbass and was on pot, valium, cocaine and beer. Of course, the police showed up and ended up hauling me away to a training school for boys. The place was rotten there were like 45 guys in the building and I hated every minute of it. That is where the court sentenced me to the next morning and there was nothing girly about that sick place.

I swear you try being a girl locked up with 45 assholes and not go crazy. I really don't think that it is necessary to tell you all about that year but it might be interesting to some people. Still, I am just going to skip along and tell it really quickly. Basically, I ended up getting sent to another lockup in Laurel, MD which only had an A and B wing. I still don't know why I was moved there but it happened. But even though it was a nicer place to be I totally fucked up. First, I spread rumors and got a riot started amongst the inmates. And then I gave some guy a leg up so that he could reach the roof and escape. Needless to say, they sent me back to training school.

But not for long because my dad pulled some strings and got me placed in a mental hospital that was really nice. I was on a hall full of problem teenagers and had my own bedroom. But then that didn't last for long either. The first incident wasn't my fault because they were giving me Thorazine and I had an allergic reaction to it. I kept having hot and cold flashes like I was sick or something. They were lining us up to take our medicines and I stood there and refused to drink the stuff. But then I messed up and took a swing at the counselor who was doling out the meds. I hit his corn cob pipe and the mouthpiece broke off and he almost swallowed it.

Another night I was acting up and they called all male aids to come and throw me into the quiet room. I wasn't quiet in there I was yelling and screaming all while a storm brewed up outside. That storm got me out of the quiet room too because lightning hit a power box right outside of the hall and by law, they couldn't keep anybody locked up during a fire. But what really screwed me up was my dysphoria was kicking and a new girl was admitted to the hall. After about a week they took us to their swimming pool and me and that girl snuck out of the building and went to my friend's house.

That wasn't the first time that I had run away from there. Once in the winter when there was about a foot and a half of snow on the ground, I had run out of the front door with no shoes on. I had gone to my best friend's house and we had then gone to some girl's house and dropped acid. I remember knocking the same ashtray over like six times. But it had started off really dangerous because in my socks I ran downhill through some woods with snow being up to three feet high on parts of the hill and I had no jacket. Anyway, let me get back to the story at hand.

I had run away with that girl and we were in my best friend's bedroom eating caffeine pills and drinking beer. At one point I had stood up and gone into the bathroom where I threw up red-colored vomit resembling if not blood. The stream of fluid was both touching the toilet bowl water and coming out of my mouth at the same time. It was a true gusher. I remember telling them that I thought that I just threw up blood. And it had been blood tainted beer that had come out of me.

There was an empty building behind my friend's house and behind it was an old shed. Earlier we had taken the shed over as a party spot and it had an army cot in it. That is where me and the girl were supposed to sleep. We did go into the shed and lay on the army cot making out and getting touchy feely. But when I went to have intercourse with her the cot tore all the way down one side and I flipped over landing on my back with her on top of me. We still made do by sleeping on the floor. Things just didn't go right during that escape.

For having run away with the girl, I was discharged from the asylum and locked up in yet another place for troubled teenaged boys. Putting a girl into a male lockup causes great amounts of dysphoria and is basically inhuman. But I have always considered myself to be a smart person because my dad always told me that I was. No harm came to me and I was just doing my time. But once again my father pulled some strings and got me out of there.

I don't really want to go on at length here about the next place so I will be brief. It was a forestry camp and there were four groups of teenaged boys living in the woods on a mountain. There was a chuck where we would all meet up for meals and get supplies such as batteries. I had run away twice from there and the second time I turned myself in to my probation officer who then filled out release papers for me. According to him I would have only been locked up for about 5 months but because of my antics it turned into a year.

Chapter#3
Goodwill Toward Me

When I had been released my dad helped me to get back into school. I was skipped ahead two grades and started in the ninth grade. I was back and all of my friends and I resumed partying on a daily basis. I would literally wake up and smoke a bowl of weed before even getting out of bed. On Christmas morning I dropped acid (Blue Unicorn) and that to me was normal. I was doing everything in my power to keep my dysphoria at bay. But the idea of being a girl was coming through in fantasies like my writing projects.

One such writing project was called "Sub Honey" and she was a really cute blonde haired teenaged girl. Her favorite thing to do was to find captive audiences like hotel clerks and then go into their workplace and sit provocatively and even mess with herself. Of course, she was an extension of me of my longing to be seen as female. I still had no idea that there were transgender people out there just transvestites. And if there is one thing that I really find unattractive it is a hairy man in a dress.

I got into the bathtub and shaved my legs, my armpits and my arms. I am blessed in that I am not a hairy person and besides some light hairs leading up to my belly button I only have like five hairs around each nipple and none on my back. Over the years the hair stopped growing back on my legs. There are a couple of patches that I need to get rid of but that's about it. Electrolysis is a big concern of mine but more on that later. For now, I want to show how easily dysphoria can pop up.

I was standing in the kitchen wearing a T-shirt and blue jeans but otherwise barefoot. Right in the middle of doing some cooking I lifted my right foot and tucked it behind my left ankle with my toes flat out upon the ground. For some reason I had an extremely feminine feeling overtake me and I was sober at the time. I remember grinning about the way that I felt and I think that I might have been blushing when I looked down into the family room at my mother. Yet another moment stuck in my memory that was a pleasure to me.

But the realization that I am still trapped in this male body creeps in and ruins those moments for me. I couldn't help but face the truth that I had hit puberty and was changing more into a masculine being all the time. Anyway, let me get back to the main story which is my having been in school. I forget how but I managed to get kicked out of the junior high that I was in despite having skipped two grades. They tried and they tried but they couldn't keep me from causing my self-destruction to win out. However, my dad stepped in and got me placed into another nearby junior high and in the same grade that I had left.

But I had entered that school as a drug dealer although I mostly kept to myself. And something new began to happen, I was laying my head in my arms and not looking at the teacher in class. The teachers complained about my actions and it got me sent to a special-ed class which I didn't like. I didn't even like to look at people anymore it was that bad. But I had no one to talk to about it either. When I had been in the asylum, I had a psychologist but I never told him anything about my gender dysphoria and truly I had never heard of it before.

All I knew was that I couldn't stop thinking that I was a girl and I hated every other aspect of my life. I can't even remember the number of girls that I had sex with but it was different for me. I was more so exploring their bodies and wishing at times that I could be one of them. Vulvas come in all sorts of shapes and sizes and I used to try and think of what I wanted mine to look like. But I wasn't a bad looking guy not by a longshot. That is how I managed to get just about any girl I saw. Anyway, I eventually had enough of the school system and dropped out.

I still remember the party at my best friend's house for graduation from high school. I sat there, bong in hand feeling like an absolute loser and I wanted to cry but that was something that I never did. Not that I'm saying that I hadn't before but it was something that I hadn't done since I was a kid. I endured that graduation party but I felt like a total fool. But I didn't feel the need to learn that crap I needed to transition but didn't yet know how. I didn't walk directly home.

In the completely opposite direction from home, I walked through a little field with a bunch of junk dumped into it. There was a big hill and going down it would start me in the right direction to get home. At the bottom of the hill were two Goodwill trailers where people would drop things off. As I was walking pat there, I noticed some hefty bags sitting outside of the trailers. I walked over and opened one up and it was filled with women's clothes. The first thing that I pulled out was the top of a nurse's outfit and it fit me perfectly. Then I dug around in the bag until I had seen like four dresses so I knew that I had to have them. It was about a mile long walk to the house so I threw the bag over my shoulder and started walking. Once I got home, I went straight to my room to try on the dresses.

They fit they all fit that donor had been just my size. There was one dress in particular with a fall floral pattern on it that had a great feeling to it. It was somehow very liberating to have my own collection of women's clothing. But that one dress must have been washed a hundred times because it was so soft it was turning me on just wearing it. I would end up keeping those dresses for years to come. Anyway, I want to get back to having gotten into so much trouble.

Even if I had been considered one of the cool kids I was suffering inside. I certainly never meant to get into so much trouble as I had. But when under the influences of so many drugs along with alcohol I could barely see what I was doing to myself much less anybody else. There is nothing cool about being arrested or doing time. It is miserable at best and filled with anxiety. I would imagine that most of the Cis boys had it easier than did I since I truly didn't belong. It is one of those situations where if you had to do it all over again you would do it differently. A had I only known then what I know now.

So, school was over and even though I did go to night school a couple of times I dropped out of that too. I can't forget the shame that I felt when my father got upset and called me a bum. I had twice taken up soccer and twice football for him because he was a sports fan. Three of those times he became the coach of the team and couldn't have been happier but to be doing it. I hadn't ever meant to affect my family through my poor drugged up choices. Things had simply spiraled out of control so what more can I really say?

After school graduation I really didn't see my old friends anymore as everyone was moving on with their lives. I would spend days just sitting in my bedroom writing rhymes and I eventually got the idea to write a book about creation and history. I had named it three times finally deciding upon Covering 4 Myself. In simple gematria that title adds up to 177 and that is just what I wanted it to do. One of the meanings that I place on that number was "1-things" as 1 equaled 1 and things equaled 77. I believe that the whole universe is but one body so one-things makes sense.

Chapter#4
Labor Intensive

After having dropped out of school I severely limited the types of jobs that I could get. But I went to a temporary agency and was assigned to a cosmetics factory. My first job was very simple I just sat at a moving conveyor with a bottle of glue in my hand. Compacts would come down the line and I would squirt a drop of glue into every one of them. It was a twelve-hour night and the breakroom coffee machine had really old tasting coffee in it. But I was at least making some money and my father seemed to approve.

Eventually they started moving me around to different positions in the factory. Some of them were quite difficult to perform as the lines moved very fast and one had to keep up while standing up for hours at a time. I really regretted having dropped out of school But I still didn't want to go and get a GED. School messed with my dysphoria too much there were always girls that I wanted to emulate. But then there were plenty of women in the factory too and one night they sat a new one across from me.

I had been put back on the line that I had started on and that woman was sitting right across from me. She was a combination of African American and American Indian with a nice smile. We talked all night for like three days and we also talked at lunch and on breaks. I got the telephone number to where she was staying in the city and called her on our day off. As it turned out she was renting a room from some woman who was currently out of town. We made plans for me to go to the house and hang out and so I went there. I had to walk a mile and then take three buses to get there.

Again, I don't want to go into too much detail about our relationship because this isn't meant to be an autobiography. But we ended up living in several different places over a three-and-a-half-year period. She was fully accepting of my crossdressing and we were both kinky together. But all of that wasn't working to curb my dysphoria and I still suffered from the same thoughts of being female inside. In the end I had to break it off with her and move back to my father's house. I don't think that he was too happy to have a twenty some year-old son living under his roof.

Crossdressing was my main outlet for my feelings along with keeping my body shaved. But the house that I lived in wasn't the right environment for what I wanted to do. Anyway, I got a job at a pizza place one that was making pizzas for stores to sell whole or by the slice. The building was across the street from the light-rail which was the train that would take you into the city and beyond. I decided one payday to take the train to North Avenue because I knew that there were a lot of drug dealers in the area. My plan was to find some women who smoked crack and buy it for them in return for letting me get dressed up and party with them.

I met a woman and told her exactly what I was after and she brought me to her girlfriend's apartment where I was given a yellow cotton dress to put on and we ordered some crack and I had a great time with the two of them. All sorts of women came and went from that apartment and some males too. But no one ever criticized my being in drag because the clothes always fit me perfectly. That and because really all that anybody cared about was getting high. I kept the job for about three years and blew all of my paychecks in that apartment.

Besides working all week and crossdressing all weekend I continued to work on the book Covering 4 Myself. Writing had become my escape to feeling trapped in the house. It was and still is an occult book even though I edited out hundreds of its pages. It had turned into a 2,065-page E-book and I couldn't see converting it to a paperback nor a hardcover book. I have edited it though and it is for sale right now. I'm sure that there are people who can see the hints of dysphoria all throughout its pages. But then that is just what I was going through when I wrote it.

Eventually my father retired and wanted to move to Pennsylvania so that my mother could be close to her family. You see he had some type of undiagnosed illness and was slowly dying like his twin brother Paul had already done. I was told to find a place to live because they were not going to allow me to move with them. I wasn't a bum I had many jobs since dropping out of school it's just that I could never keep them and I blame depression, the dysphoria. Anyway, I had to move and I only had a month to find a place to live. I don't have a clue as to why but I ended up living in Fell's Point in downtown Baltimore city.

I wanted to work where they paid the most to a dropout so that would be the huge factory/warehouse bakery down the street from me. At first, they said that they weren't hiring but I talked to my father and he said to go there every day until they hired me. It took about two or three weeks but they hired me and I was gainfully employed. And my apartment was back in an alley where nobody could see so I could wear whatever I wanted. But I was getting tired of wearing the nurse's old clothes I wanted new threads. It turned out that there was a women's used dress shop right around the corner from me.

I remember walking in there and leafing through some dresses but it felt funny to me like the woman working there was not into my being there. I promptly left and went home where I decided that it was all in my head and she probably just wanted my business. I didn't go back and buy anything but it became a fantasy of mine to be in that shop. I imagined going in there and trying on dozens of dresses and asking her what she thought about each one. But even though I loved the idea I never did go back there and do it.

They had moved me from off of the breadline to a machine off on its own called the Swat. A very fast paced machine that really stressed me out and eventually caused me to quit the job. Either that or the fact that I was sitting home in the bathtub smoking crack when I should have been at work. But I think that I had made the choice to smoke the crack and skip work intentionally because of the stress that the machine was causing me. It was just such a relaxing bath with a bunch of cocaine to smoke and beer to drink as well. I have always loved to take really long baths and read or party in the tub.

This is when my story gets really tricky because I had met my future wife. But to be honest with you I believe that I had already seen her in a dream. I had a dream in which I was standing looking at my full-length mirror just where it was in reality at the foot of my bed in Timonium. The year was 1995. There was no reflection of me in the mirror but I could clearly see the bed behind where I stood. And there upon my pillow was a bunch of black hair. I knew by the shape of the head that a woman was laying in my bed so I turned around to face her.

I had turned around and placed my right leg knee down upon the bed and just stared at her head. Then she looked up for a moment and lay back down. Next, she sat up and pulled her right leg out from the covers and placed her foot upon my right hand which was upon my knee. Her foot felt extremely soft I remember that about the dream. Anyway, without getting into the whole thing I'll jump a little ahead. Up until then everything was exactly the way my room was set up in reality.

Then she pointed to the floor and the scene changed to the back of a girl with long black hair listening to a Walkman radio with headphones. It had been yellow. One night I met a long black-haired Chinese woman in Fell's Point and we talked for a while. Days later when I walked home, I saw her standing waiting for me at my gate at around 10:45 p.m. I let her in and then we ended up living together in a nearby house. After separating for some time, we finally got back together and got married in a courthouse. Anyway, she owned a yellow Walkman with yellow headphones.

My wife knew that I liked to cross-dress but I really didn't like to do it around her. After getting married my mother gave us $9,000 as a wedding present and I held onto it. I wanted to be wearing dresses and partying with women but I had a falling out with my old connection so I drove into the city looking for a crack addicted female to give me a place to go. That turned out to be really easy and I was partying in a house with a woman who just wanted some heroin and didn't really care about what I was doing. One thing that I wasn't doing was having sex with any of them. I knew better than to do that.

My wife had to wonder where I kept going but she never said anything about it. She probably thought that I was having an affair with someone. At any rate the money soon dried up and she served me with divorce papers. With her gone I couldn't afford the apartment on my own so I called my mother. My father had passed away back in 1997 and this was like 2003. She heard me out and told me that I could have the guest room in the house in Pa. I packed up and moved there and stayed for years. During the time that I lived there I used to chat a lot on Yahoo Chat and met quite a few people through it as well.

One of them lived all the way up in New York but she would come and visit me on the weekends and party. I realize that I am leaving a lot out of this book and have been doing so on purpose. Again, this wasn't meant to be an autobiography. It is to show how dysphoria has basically ruined my life time after time. But it (the dysphoria) is so wrapped up in my daily life that I can't help but include multitudes of real time events to explain it. And it isn't depression even though they medicated me for that. They had told me that the medication could cause breast growth in males and it made me want more of it. Needless to say, they took me off of it and put me on something else.

Anyway, there I was with this really cool girlfriend from New York when my mother took ill and died. I was devastated and about to become homeless as well. But my friend from New York came to the funeral and told me that I could stay with her until I got on my feet. I was truly grateful and I packed up the car and headed for New York. Later the two of us went back to Pennsylvania and gathered all of my stuff and put it into a couple of storage units. Then we went back to New York.

I got a job at a country club as a dishwasher so I wasn't just sitting on my ass all day. And maybe it is because of all of the stress that I have had to endure throughout my life or not but I am a little crazy. I got the first part of my inheritance in the form of stock shares that I sold for $7,000. I left my girlfriend for no real reason and drove to Miami where I stayed until the day, I was down to $120. I drove back to New York and she let me in. It wasn't like we hadn't stayed friends we used to talk on the phone like every day when I was in Florida. And I believe she thinks that I am a little crazy too.

The day after I had gotten back from squandering $7,000 a letter came for me. The house had sold in Pennsylvania and my share of the money was in a check in that envelope. It was for $38,000 and I had enough money to do one heck of a lot of transitioning right there. But I still didn't even know about transgender things such as transitioning. I have since fantasized having it to do over and using the whole $45,000 to become as female as possible. Add having a job to that money and I could have gone on HRT, gotten FFS, a boob job and voice surgery too. But I would still need SRS or bottom surgery.

Anyway, I was ignorant too my options at the time and what mattered to me was getting my belongings out of storage. I left most of my stuff in the attic in New York and drove my car back to Pennsylvania to get my stuff out of storage. I was living in a motel when I met this woman online and she came to see me. We hit it off and she told me that there was an empty two-bedroom apartment right next to hers and that she would help me move my things from the storage to the apartment. I went the next day and got the apartment knowing that I needed the second bedroom for all of the extraneous stuff that I had brought from my mother's house.

I rented a truck and that woman my new neighbor helped me to load and unload it all into the new apartment. I was able to make a very cozy bedroom, a functional bathroom and kitchen and a comfortable living room. The rest of the stuff all got put into the second bedroom where it just fit. I had two and three of a lot of things because of my marriage and my mother's having passed away. In short, I had too much stuff but some of it did serve as backup in case something else would break. All in all, I was very happy with how the place turned out.

I was having relations with the woman who had helped me but we were also friends and went out to eat together and things like that. The first year there I stayed drunk and played video games, watched TV and bathed a lot. I stayed in the bathtub for an entire day once watching The Walking Dead on Net-Flix. I had a laptop and two PC's. But staying drunk got old and I wasn't seeing as much of that woman because she was having an affair with somebody else. I started to get dysphoric all over again because I had to shave my face and legs all the time. And I was starting to get really lonely.

Back when I lived at my mother's house, I had a My Space account and on there I had a friend that used to chat with me all the time. I hadn't used the site since my mother died and couldn't remember my password to log in nor my old email. But then I found an old notebook and there was the password so I logged in and started to check my mail. There were like some thousand or so messages on there and I started deleting them all. However, out of the corner of my eye I noticed a message from the woman that I had used to chat with all the time.

I contacted her and she sent me a phone number to call her. We talked for hours and eventually I told her that she could come and live with me. Her ex-boyfriend had broken up with her and had moved her to a different state into a one room miniature apartment. She took me up on my offer and I drove down there to pick her up. The part that I didn't like was that I had to pay her last months rent to get her out of there. She lived off of SSI because she had an identity disorder so there was money coming to her for her. I still had over $20,000. But I was just surviving and being a total drunk while doing so. She thought that it would be a good idea for me to get a job which is exactly what I hurried up and did.

I had simply gone to a temp agency and they had placed me in a job because the bitch that was training me didn't like me. It turned out that I had once dated a friend of hers. They placed me into another job and I stayed for two days in that candy factory but I hated it. I quit that job and went to another temp agency and got hired at a place that I had worked before when my mother was still alive. That job was okay it was four nights on and four nights off at twelve hours a day. The money paid my rent and not my inheritance for a change.

But I was spending over a thousand dollars a month on other bills, liquor and beer. The cool thing was is that the woman who had moved in had food stamps and liked to go shopping. She also liked to cook and she could do so well so I was eating really good for a change. I just realized that I have left out an important part of my crossdressing fixation. I'll have to write it into the next paragraph because I think it counts for something. And yes, the woman that moved in with me knew all about my wanting to be female. But I still didn't know how to just say that I was.

All the way back to when I was married, I had used to put address in the trunk of my car and drive around looking for places to walk around in drag. No makeup and no knowledge about applying any. All that I wanted was my face and legs shaved and to be barefoot when I would put on a dress. I never did go in for trying on heels, I'm more the small leather boots type. But I would drive out into the middle of nowhere like at powerlines and then change and walk for a while. I especially liked walking on grass or through puddles.

Anyway, after a year and some had passed, I started to run out of my inheritance. I shouldn't have told that woman but one day after quitting my job we got an eviction notice on the door. She was livid and said that she was going to her sisters for Christmas. I didn't think that she would come back and after three weeks it proved to be the case. There was an insurance policy that paid me $316 a month and there was over a year left on it. I sent them a letter claiming that I was about to be homeless if I couldn't pay the rent and could I please have the balance of the annuity.

The graced me with the full amount owed to mesome $8,000 and I paid my landlord. Then I called that woman and told her about it and that I was planning on moving out of Pennsylvania and starting over. She came back like two days later and we began hunting for a new place to live online the next day. We found a small apartment in Ohio for only $550 a month and no utilities. But it was small and I had all of that stuff in the second bedroom to get rid of. Some of it I put online for sale really cheap and the rest I put for free. People were knocking on the door all day and we eventually got rid of about fifty percent of my belongings.

My dysphoria wasn't my biggest problem but keeping hold of my friend was. I figured that moving to Ohio would be the right thing to do if I wanted her to stick around. We rented a truck and loaded it up right to the very back of it. I had a tow hitch for my car and we were about to be on our way. But the guy at the truck place noticed something that I didn't even know and that was that my driver's license had expired. I had to go right away to get that taken care of but I also had to park at a shopping center across the street so that they wouldn't know that I drove there.

It was snowing when we left and it continued to all the way into Ohio. It was a pretty long truck and I had a car behind it so I had to be extra careful with my driving. But we finally pulled into the parking lot where the apartment was and began to unpack the truck. She was a great helper and we got the job done in a couple of hours. The apartment looked like a bomb had exploded in it but everything was in there. We returned the truck and took a cab back then went right to bed. I remember how exhausted I was from all that.

This was when my life took a turn for the better as far as I was concerned. After totally putting everything in its place we had a functional apartment and went food shopping. Two weeks later I was working fulltime for Walmart stocking grocery shelves on the graveyard shift. There was a nice wooden deck in the back of the two-story apartment and I bought plastic chairs and put them out there. I also bought a chopping block cabinet set and put it next to the stove. Then I bought shelves for the bathroom and a hanging rack to put things on in the shower, there was no tub.

That's the one thing that I didn't like about the place it didn't have a bathtub. But I was fulltime in wearing dresses while we lived there except when sitting out on the deck. I simply didn't want to be seen by anybody around that small mostly vacation town. Most of the neighbors were bikers and I didn't think that they would approve. I would sometimes change my clothes five or six times a day if not more. But my girlfriend kept my toes polished black which was really cool of her to do for me. I still hadn't heard about HRT nor any things concerning transitioning into a female bodily.

Had I only opened my eyes I would have had an easy time of it back then. That is back when I first got my inheritance. But I got tired of that fantasy because it always left me with regrets. Now, I'd bet that you are wondering what went wrong next. Well, this turns into the worst time of my life to date but not quite yet it didn't. We lived in that little apartment with three premium cable channels, Net-Flix, her laptop and my PC to keep us occupied. And about a year went by without any problems arising.

But even though I was continually dressing how I wanted to both in the apartment and out in far away places things were getting financially messed up. I kept buying thirty packs of beer and drinking like sixteen beers a day if not more. And even though I don't now back then I used to smoke cigarettes which cost a fortune. So, between the cable bill, cigarettes and beer I was blowing all of my money. She bought most of the food and put up most of the rent money. The food with food stamps and the rent was paid in cash and I only paid a little of it.

My dysmorphia had gotten really bad and I started thinking that all kinds of people knew that I was really a girl. Around the apartment, at work and when we would go shopping. And I knew that I was blushing more than usual and it bothered the heck out of me. I had become highly paranoid about my identity but had to carry on as usual. One thing that I thought would help was if I wrote a book so I started writing one about the Anti-Christ. That was a horrible mistake as it took me to a very dark place inside. And I was researching on You-Tube but failed to see any transgender videos.

Anyway, I would get out of bed sober and go straight to work and then crack a beer as soon as I got home. How was I supposed to get any writing done when I was drunk all of the time? And writing about the Anti-Christ was the worst idea I ever had. I had scribbled notes on paper and notes on my PC and even a few paragraphs got done but they were crazily written. One day I just went off and started screaming and yelling at the computer. The police came and I ended up shutting up for the rest of the day. But then maybe two weeks later I started yelling again but this time my girlfriend told me to stop and come watch TV with her.

I should have gone into the other room with her but I was in a stupor and I didn't. My drunk ass had quit yelling but I didn't go and join her. Little did I know she had called her sister and told her what was up. I went to bed as usual and too got up and went to work. However, when I got home, she had packed her things and left with her sister while I had been at work. Worst of all she took the rent money with her. It was due the next day and I had no time to work for the money and had only $50 to my name. My landlady came by the next day to collect the rent and I told her that my girlfriend ran off with it.

I got paid every two weeks and had just gotten paid and spent it that week. The cable was paid for the month but I had to buy food and there were my addictions smoking and drinking. Not to mention gas as my job was a 35-minute drive each way. And there I was knowing that in two weeks I wouldn't have enough to pay them and would need money myself anyway. I started selling things like two antique lamps that I owned which I only got $75 for. And that money went straight to cigarettes and beer. I was so stressed out that I doubt that I was even dysphoric that week.

Anyway, I overslept and missed a night of work. Then there was a huge storm and I was on my way to work when the car slid off the road and into a ditch. I got soaked but I got the car out and turned around and went home to change. But my other clothes were dirty and I ended up just staying home that night. I forget how it happened but I missed a third night and lost the job. I was screwed there really weren't any other jobs out there. And now I certainly wouldn't have their money. I got really paranoid and dysphoric as well. I decided that I had better leave before they had me locked out of the apartment with nothing but the clothes on my back.

Chapter#5
Homelessness

I was in one of the worst mental states of my life with dysphoria, fear, loneliness, paranoia and regrets. I bought some beer with the last of my money and went back to the apartment to pack whatever I could into my car. I wasn't thinking right at the time but was piling things onto the floor that I wanted to take with me. I owned thousands of dollars-worth of books but only grabbed like three of them, o how to about repairing computers, a magical spell book and I forget the other one. I had four large boxes filled with paper which was years-worth of handwritten original Covering 4 Myself work. I should have left them but I put them into the car.

Those four boxes took up most of the space in the car and I had already typed the whole book onto my PC anyway. I also have thousands worth of paintings and those I was able to fit into the back seat of the car. I only had a small Hyundai Accent to work with so there wasn't much room. Of course, I took my PC monitor and all. The PC was on my passenger seat right next to me along with a few other items. I had filled the trunk, backseat and front passenger side until the car could hold no more. I kept thinking that people were coming to try to stop me and I was totally paranoid at the time.

But no one ever showed up and I climbed into the car realizing that I couldn't even put the seat back because of all the stuff in the back. And my only plan was to drive to Timonium and star over. I had left thousands of dollars-worth of belongings behind and as I drove away, I felt utterly defeated. There was some gas in the car but I was out of cash. Like I said I wasn't thinking right. All I could think about were regrets about having lost the job because I could have worked my way out of the situation.

Hours went by and it had gotten dark as I was driving on red lit empty. I was so afraid to run out of gas because I couldn't afford towing and yard costs and would lose everything that I had left. I pulled into some small town and was the only car in sight as I drove into the gas station which was closed. But the pumps were on so I got out and stuck my debit card into the pump and it gave me $25 worth of gas. That was it I had blown out my bankcard and really, I only had like $3 in there the rest was given to me as an overdraft.

So now my bankcard was no good unless I could pay back the money it just gave me. But that had filled my tank and my Accent got great milage so that I was able to drive all the way to Timonium. I pulled into a strip-mall and parked the car right under a surveillance camera on a Mars super market. It seemed like the safest place to put the car so that nobody would touch it. And of course, I had brought all of my dresses folded up in a lawn and leaf bag. On top of that bag and clearly visible was my white bow as in bow and arrows only without the arrows.

I had very little gas left and no money to buy food with it was terrifying. I had never been homeless before and didn't know how to begin it seemed like I was going to die out there. I had to sleep sitting straight up because I couldn't move the seat at all. But I crashed from all of the stress and fell right to sleep anyway. In the morning my plan was to walk to the Cockeysville library and use one of their computers to look for any type of a job or a place to stay. It would take around an hour to walk there from where I was parked.

I went to the library but I didn't find anything job wise nor any place to stay. There were no shelters in that part of the county so I just left there feeling discouraged. The library was up on a hill overlooking a school and part of a neighborhood. Looking down I could see York-road which is where I planned to go next. But as I was nearing the road, I saw a man pushing an augur around and decided to stop and talk to him. He was obviously building a fence as there were poles laying all over the ground and an augur to dig holes with.

I had asked him if he needed any help and he told me that his friend couldn't make it that day so yes, he needed help. He said that he was a Deacon and was building the fence for a newlywed couple. He offered to pay me $15 an hour and I was elated. After telling him that I had just become homeless he stopped working and took me to a fast-food place and bought me a meal. That night I ate Chinese food and had a six pack of beer in my cramped car. He had paid me for the day and said to come

26

back tomorrow. I couldn't believe my luck although I didn't believe it was luck at all.

The job lasted for another three days and I had a good bit of money for food and gas. After that God send, I decided to start going to AA meetings and maybe sober up. I was out driving around and I saw a little Methodist church and pulled in there to enquire about meeting. The pastor and his wife were both there working on painting a sign and I introduced myself and told them about my situation. He gave me a schedule and told me that they had meetings daily there. That would give me a chance to meet some people and maybe get some tips about finding work or a place to stay.

I had attended every meeting that they had there that week plus having gone to other meetings which I had learned about from my schedule. And I forget how but somehow, I ended up living at the Walmart parking lot out near the corner away from most other cars. I had tried to get a job there but they weren't hiring. I would only be there at night and it was a 24-hour store. Then I made a really smart move I rented a storage unit in Timonium for $80 for two months and unpacked the car into it.

Finally, I was able to put down the car seat and get some decent sleep. I had kept a couple of dresses with me and I would put one on in the car before getting under my blanket to go to sleep. But I would wake up dysphoric because of the stubble on my face. Anyway, I was still alive and it had been about three weeks since I had left Ohio. And I never felt guilty about the way that I left because I had left thousands of dollars-worth of stuff behind.

One night during an AA meeting at the Methodist church I was outside smoking a cigarette when the Pastor pulled up. He told me that I was just who he had been looking for and then told me that he was going to let me sleep in the basement of the church where meetings were held. He said that he had brought an airbed that I could simply inflate and then deflate in the morning. I couldn't believe it I was going to be staying inside and with a bathroom down there too. That night after everyone had left, I set up the airbed and got a decent night of sleep.

In the morning I deflated the bed and stuck it under a table in the back of the room along with a bag of my clothes. But I kept my dresses in the trunk of my car just in case anybody had prying eyes. I walked into all sorts of places trying to find work but got frowned on a lot for being honest about my situation. But then the manager of a restaurant offered me an under the table job washing dishes and I took it. So, I had a job, a place to sleep indoors and gas for my car. But there was a 24-hour laundromat and I started hanging out in it and talking with the employees. In there they had a bathroom and I could do my laundry and watch the news on TV.

Anyway, dysphoria is a very real and disturbing illness that can lead to all sorts of problems. There is a non-profit organization that has an outreach program for the homeless so I called them. Someone had driven out to meet me in Cockeysville and took me to a house in Towson owned by the organization that allowed homeless people to do their laundry there, watch TV and play cards. Otherwise, they were there to help assist a person in getting on food stamps and if diagnosed with an illness then on SSI. On another day I was taken to a hospital and after going there several times they diagnosed me with a mental illness.

I got a free government phone a really cheap old one and had filled out an application for SSI benefits. There was just so much positive change thanks to that organization. But I started to get dysphoric as I sobered up so I started drinking again and lost the dishwashing job. Nevertheless, I got a job working in the cosmetics factory that I had worked in when I was a teenager. That was a decent paying job and it was fulltime as well. But some of the church elders were worried that after thirty days I would have squatters-rights so they put me out of the church.

I was still attending Sunday service and AA meetings but no more did I sleep there. That was terrible I had to go back to living at Walmart. I wasn't the only homeless person in Cockeysville there were at least six of us at any one time. I had somewhat become friends with a couple of them and we would hang out in various places and drink together. And I kept hearing in my head that I was a girl and didn't belong there. Anyway, there was also a Lutheran church that used to give me kitchen rights and feed me box dinners for lunch. They were also where one of the AA meetings took place.

And the greatest gift of all came from a female Pastor at a church that I had stopped into seeking assistance in any way I could get it. There were three churches in a row and one was an old historic site. She agreed to let me take my stuff out of storage and put it into the old church. That saved me a lot of money and my things were basically safe in there. That was another church that had AA meetings. I was slowly drinking less beer because I truly did want to sober up. But it wasn't easy because all these feelings would come rushing in when I wasn't drinking for any substantial period of time.

I had lost the job at the cosmetics factory due to not showing up on time three different times. Once it was because a T-shirt had fallen between the hammer and the bell on my little alarm clock so I was twenty minutes late. They didn't allow lateness at all there. Then there was another church which used to give me $25 and it too was an AA location. I had resorted to smoking these cigarlike cigarettes which came in grape flavor. They were very cheap so I could buy a couple packs of those and get gas too. Meanwhile I had let my car insurance lapse because I just couldn't pay it.

Then one day I got pulled over by a police officer and he told me that the sticker on my license tag was expired and to fix the situation. I couldn't afford to do anything about insurance or the sticker so I parked my car at Walmart and didn't drive it anymore. I had to walk most places but sometimes was able to take a bus. Anyway, I had made friends with a guy at an AA meeting and started hanging round his house even sleeping on the couch when his sister would go out of town. It was her house but she had a boyfriend in another state. And he lived on the same street as the Pastor who had let me stay on the airbed in his church.

But another winter was coming and I had been homeless for over a year and my car had broken down in the Walmart parking lot. Okay so I had nowhere to sleep without freezing. That organization told me about a homeless shelter and I was to go there and meet with someone in three days. The good thing was that my friend's sister was out of town for the week so I was sleeping on the couch for those three days while waiting. At that point I had been sober for over two months. It hadn't been easy being sober but I was getting serious about my life.

I only got $100 when my car was towed away but then it didn't even run, the transmission was messed up and the trunk broken open. After three days of a geek out to the show Ancient Aliens I was finally on my way to the homeless shelter. I had to take all sorts of buses to get there but when I did the guy checked me right in. It was a pretty decent shelter so I say but it was the first that I have ever entered. There was a rec-room, a cafeteria and two large rooms full of bunk beds. I took a shower and was given a top bunk in the back corner of the room.

The shelter was on the grounds of a mental hospital and about a ten-minute walk to town. Sometimes they would bus us into town and other times we would walk. I say we because I rely went out alone. Well, in the beginning I had but I ended up making a friend or two along the way and hung out with them. The organization that was helping me was trying to place me into some sort of housing for the mentally ill situation but it backfired because of my record. In the end they interviewed me to go and live in one of their houses and join their community.

I was accepted and one of the homeless outreach people drove me to the old church to pick up my belongings. It was all moved into a three-bedroom house in a county and I had the master bedroom with one other guy living down the hall. Soon a third man moved in and then the house was full. I had used to sleep in dresses, mainly my T-shirt dress up until the new guy came and then I stopped crossdressing completely. He used to come to my door a lot and I didn't like to yell through it.

They have a big building where they hold classes and have other programs like for drug and alcohol addicts. We used to be bused there five days a week for the day and had breakfast and lunch too. But that all changed with Covid-19 and the place was closed. It has since opened but for only for like an hour and only three days a week. And you have to have been fully vaccinated to attend and I didn't get any shots. I don't believe in the vaccine so I have been staying home for over two years now working on my writing.

I would like to get more into the topic of transitioning and going over what I've learned about it. With all of this time on my hands I have spent a couple hundred hours at least learning about transitioning. I know now what I must do and I plan to do it all the very best that I can.

Chapter#6
Unfolding the Great Discovery

I don't remember when I first took notice of it but the way to transition became something that I was finally aware of. I had been on You-Tube and had caught sight of something like MTF transitions. I watched eagerly and went down the list one at a time viewing them. It was probably the coolest discovery of my lifetime. I especially like the HRT timelines that are on there, they really gave me hope. But what am I talking about with these abbreviations? I will get into all of that soon enough. For now, I want to break down my personal needs.

I need to be a successful enough author to have a few surgeries performed. And that is no joke as these are very costly procedures. Starting with HRT or Hormone Replacement Therapy. I'm not going to get into the hormone blockers for teens in here as I am not a teen and require a different process. But basically, you need to be on something that stops the flow of testosterone in your body. That and you need to replace the testosterone with estrogen. That is how replacement therapy works. You take both a testosterone blocker and estrogen.

As I write this, I am waiting to go to my first endocrinologist appointment which is three months from now. I have yet to start the process and all that I write comes from research that I've done online and too my LGBTQ therapist. But by the time this book is published I should be on HRT. The hard thing for me right now is getting electrolysis in my area and too affording it. That is when they permanently remove all of the hairs from your mustache and beard. I might have to put it off for a while longer. But shaving is big on my dysphoria list because I absolutely hate shaving my face.

And then there is FFS or Facial Femininization Surgery which is something that I am craving. There are a number of procedures that can be done to the male face to feminize it. I plan on having my chin rounded, my lips made bigger, my nose thinned, my brow bone reduced, my eyebrows lifted, my jaw worked on and my apple shaved. That is about $16,000 worth of work and I really need to sell a lot of books to get to that point. Am I being unrealistic in today's economy? I don't believe so I have great faith in my work.

Something that I both watched and carefully listened to was a doctor from UCLA talking about voice feminization. He explained the procedure that they use and then played a before and after recording of the patient's voice. It completely blew my mind to hear how feminine the voice had become. Since then, I have learned that they usually o it differently on the east coast but with the same results. That one costs around $7,000. It I already up to $23,000 just for the two surgeries and I still need my facial hair removed and breast augmentation.

Breast augmentation is a must and can cost as much as $10,000. HRT only gives people like size A breasts and they are too small for my frame. I don't really want big breasts just ones that fir into my rather small bodily frame. I think that a C-cup would do just fine. You know that I am still kicking myself over squandering my $45,000 inheritance. I could have at least gotten the first three operations out of the way. But you live and you learn and I just happened to have learned the hard way. However, after having been sober now for over seven years and after quitting smoking too I believe that I have the potential to make my dream come true.

So, let's just say that I have been on HRT for nearly a year and I'm able to afford FFS then I'll get it done. The estrogen will have already made me more feminine and the surgery once it heals on my face will make me look much, much more feminine yet. But I will still need electrolysis to permanently remove the unwanted facial hair. I don't feel like rocking a beard while having a feminine face. That, may be okay for some but it gets my dysphoria going just thinking about it. Now, let's say that I'm on HRT, had electrolysis and FFS but must decide between vocal feminization and breast augmentation.

For me it is a no brainer because I have a deep voice and it will probably out me when I speak. To be pass is to pass as a female to be outed is to have someone become aware that you are transgender. I might be dysphoric over my breast size but I would still go for the voice surgery first. What really got my dysphoria going was watching Cis women trying to show how to raise your pitch through voice training. I just couldn't hit that E sound and neither could I hum. I admit that after smoking for thirty years I have probably damaged my voice. But I'll put my money where my mouth is and go for surgery to help and correct my pitch.

So, say that I'm finally pass with no facial hair, softer skin, a higher pitched voice and nice breasts to go along with my newly feminized face. But what about my penis and testicles? Obviously, I'm going to want to have bottom surgery or SRS which is Sexual Reassignment Surgery. I will want to have my penis turned into a vulva and too, have a canal or vagina. And with no more testicles producing testosterone I probably won't have to take blockers anymore. It would be fantastic to finally have a vulva between my legs.

In some countries their citizens get most of this surgery for free after years of counseling. In America it is more like $1200 to $1500 for HRT unless your insurance covers it. $16,000 for facial feminization surgery. $7,000 for vocal surgery. Around $10,000 for breast augmentation. $1200 to 2,000 for electrolysis. And up to 30,000 for bottom surgery. Or around $66.500 for the whole lot. I don't know about you but for me as I typed this that is quite a lot of money. I could pay rent for years with money like that.

But I've undertaken this venture so I need all the support that I can possibly get. Sometimes I feel that I'm just paying to have book covers made and it is getting me nowhere and then all of the sudden I hit a windfall. But there are other expenses like makeup and clothing. I already own a pretty significant wardrobe but have yet to learn the art of applying makeup. However, I have watched some video tutorials on the subject and will continue to do so. The internet is an important tool for your transition. On it you can find just about anything that you would ever need to know.

I have seen large burly men transition into feminine creatures and the before and after pictures are amazing. I can hardly wait to see how I turn out once I have completed my own transition. And with my dysphoria it is all or nothing for me. My goal is not to take as long as five years to transition but to accomplish it in like three. That to me is a doable timeframe and I am hellbent on completing it. I so desire to be pass that it isn't funny. I really am tired of suffering in this life. If you are a nice person than wish me a fast and beautiful transition. I really do appreciate nice people.

The End

See below for other books written by this author

Elizabeth Bathory 177

I only want to hurt you, to tear you apart
I only want to drain the blood from your heart
To hear each drip and see each drop
First to sip and then to sop

Bather in blood, lesbian, murderer, tiger, torturer, vampire, werewolf and witch.
All titles of the infamous Countess Elizabeth Bathory of Hungary.
Now read about the woman called the most prolific female serial killer
By the Guinness World book of records.
And again, enjoy yourself.

The One-Eyed Alien Baby vampire

This is an action-packed book.
It was written under the pen name Roderick Naughton.
With over 70 individual kills it is a thriller.
It is a haunting piece of vampire lore.
So again, enjoy yourself.

Cold Toes
Vampire

This book is coming out on October 31st 2022.
Lisa a twelve-year-old girl takes to worshiping an ancient Egyptian Goddess named Bat.
When she turns thirteen everything in her life changes as she has to encounter the undead.
Wickedness abounds upon the earth and Lisa is inexorably caught up in it.
Her Wiccan priestess mother helps her in battling the demons which she must face.
But in the end her calling is to go to Egypt in search of an amulet belonging to the Goddess Bat.
Due to too much time already taken off from work her mother is unable to go with her.
Will Lisa be picked up by Egyptian authorities as a child in need of supervision?
Her mother has booked her a ten-day Nile cruise and that is all the time she has to find the amulet.

Covering 4 Myself

1234
Follow the path dark as may be
Unto the gate a demon you'll see
Into the realm of confusion supreme
Myth and theology clash as a dream

Fictional Vampire

What do an ex-skinhead, a practicing Satanist, a candy shop girl and a heroin addict have in common? How about drunks and drug addicts, stripers and prostitutes? Or even a serial killer hidden within this book? They all have to do with one Moses Theodore Ramsey, aka Motor within this coming-of-age tale with many twists and turns. Follow Motor's life as it spirals out of control leading him down some of the darkest times to be imagined.

The Universal Mind
(Creator)
Havens and Shell

Post-Earth Reality

The truth about what is called God
The truth about what is called Heaven
The truth about what is called Hell
And what happened to this Earth
The answers that you have been looking for

www.ingramcontent.com/pod-product-compliance
Lightning Source LLC
Chambersburg PA
CBHW050352290526
45785CB00006B/2746